To My Son,
The
Teen-Age
Driver

Books by Henry Gregor Felsen

LETTERS TO A TEEN-AGE SON
ANYONE FOR CUB SCOUTS?
BERTIE COMES THROUGH
BERTIE MAKES A BREAK
BERTIE TAKES CARE
BOY GETS CAR
THE BOY WHO DISCOVERED THE EARTH
THE COMPANY OWNS THE TOOLS
CRASH CLUB
CUB SCOUT AT LAST
CUP OF FURY
DAVEY LOGAN, INTERNE
DR., IT TICKLES
FEVER HEAT
FLYING CORRESPONDENT
HE'S IN SUBMARINES NOW
HE'S IN THE COAST GUARD NOW
HOT ROD
JUNGLE HIGHWAY
NAVY DIVER
PILOTS ALL
SOME FOLLOW THE SEA
STREET ROD
STRUGGLE IS OUR BROTHER
SUBMARINE SAILOR
TWO AND THE TOWN

To My Son, The Teen-Age Driver

302961E

by Henry Gregor Felsen

Dodd, Mead & Company NEW YORK

TO MY SON,

WHO IS NOW

THE 20-YEAR-OLD

RACING DRIVER

CONTENTS

I

You, Who Are About to Drive

MY SON
Dan and I began talking seriously about cars and driving when he was about twelve years old and just becoming addicted to hot rods. The talks continued through the high school years, when his one ambition in life was to

be a racing driver.

Now he is nineteen—a month away from being twenty—and we still discuss cars and driving, but now we do it in letters because he is a Marine, and far from home. And now he talks about the kind of car he'd like to have when he returns to college—something that provides dependable transportation and doesn't use too much gas.

To the best of my knowledge (no parent ever knows everything), Dan went through his teen-age years without a ticket or an accident. I have reason to believe that my words helped him live in peace and understanding with his car and his community. Perhaps the same words can do as much for you.

II
The Longest Ride in Your Life

A COUPLE
of weeks ago you reached your sixteenth birthday.

A few days later you began—then completed—a driver-training course.

This morning you passed your state driving test.

This afternoon you took my car for your first solo drive.

This afternoon, for the first time in our lives, I proudly watched you drive away alone, in sole command of two tons of machinery, solely responsible for the behavior of two hundred and fifty horsepower. Your trip took you eight blocks from home and eight blocks back. I wonder if you know how far that trip really took you—not only from where I stood, but from your own self of yesterday. You may never take a longer ride than this.

You seemed surprised that I let you use my car the first time you asked for it. Surprised that I would trust you to drive it alone. Yet how could I, without good reason, deny you a trust which the community has in you?

To the highway patrol examiner you were just another boy taking the test. He had no personal feelings toward you, no private reason to pass or fail you. He judged you solely on your performance. And, when you satisfied this official examiner that you were competent to drive, and received an adult's driving license, it became my duty to go along—not with *your* claim that you were competent to drive alone, but with *his*.

I trust you to drive alone now just as I will have to trust you—when the law says you are old enough—to vote or marry without my consent, assistance, or direction.

You know, it is a good thing for parents as well as children that these decisions are made by law. We parents are so close to our children, so biased for or prejudiced against, so affected by emotion, that it is difficult for us to see them objectively as people. If driving, for example, were strictly a family affair, some children would be driving cars when they were nine years old, and some denied the wheel when they were nineteen. We need the help of the community, through law, to determine when our children are (or should be) ready to receive certain adult privileges and to take on certain adult responsibilities.

This is how you grow up and away from me, one sudden step at a time. Today, as yesterday, you are still in my care, still a high school boy, still a child in many ways. But today, unlike yesterday, you have the legal right to drive a car by yourself, on any road you choose. And, as of today, in your new role as driver, the world you travel through views and accepts you as a man.

I trust you alone in a car because the time has come when the community says I must trust you. I trust you because you are my son, and I want to trust you. I trust you because I know you want to be trustworthy.

I say this and I mean it, yet there is a question in my mind that seems to contradict everything I have said about trusting you. It is this: The community believes you are an adult behind the wheel, and I believe you are an adult behind the wheel. How long will it take before *you* believe that you are an adult behind the wheel?

What I wonder is, how long will it take before your immediate, instinctive actions and reactions as a driver are those of a man, and not a boy? Your right to drive, your personal freedom, your life, may depend on how soon you can come up with the answer to this question.

III

A Boy on Foot
Is a Man on Wheels

MANY TIMES, these past few years, you have complained that you were not being treated like an adult. Now, as a driver, you will be treated like an adult —*whether you like it or not!*

I have heard many teen-age drivers complain that the police picked on them because they were kids. I'm sure this does happen, perhaps more than it should. But most of the time the reverse is true. The reason the police *seem* to pick on young drivers is because they are *not* kids when they drive, and cannot be permitted to act like kids.

The truth is that you, like any other new driver, are in a tough spot. For when the community gave you your license this morning, it made a demand on you that you cannot possibly meet.

All your life until today you have been learning to be a boy in a man's world. Even now, 99 per cent of your life must be lived as a boy in a man's world. But as of today the community demands that, in the 1 per cent of your life that you are a driver, you *immediately* act and think like a man.

This demand is made on you the instant you accept your license. I know you are more than willing to do this. Probably, you think you do. But you cannot, no matter how hard you try, shake off in an instant the habits, outlooks and attitudes of a lifetime—even if that lifetime is only sixteen years.

I will illustrate what I mean with two incidents out of your life.

Today you are a fairly big and rugged boy, and you know it. But you were a big and rugged boy for some time before you could be convinced of that fact.

When you began elementary school, you were one of the youngest and smallest boys in your class, and you remained small for several years. And that, I suppose, became your own normal picture of yourself.

Suddenly, there came a year when you grew several inches taller and put on forty pounds of weight, and you became one of the big boys. Now, although you could stand in front of the mirror and see the change, you did not recognize it. You continued referring to smaller friends as being bigger than you were, and thinking of yourself as smaller and weaker than they.

I, being a little further away from you than yourself, saw the change, and I began to treat you like a bigger, stronger boy. Since you didn't see yourself the way I saw you, we had our troubles getting together. As far as you were concerned, I was talking about a stranger.

In a way you were right. I was talking to the boy I saw on the outside, but not to the one who lived beneath that skin. I am sure it seemed to you I was asking things of you that were above and beyond your ability to perform. And it took some time before you could believe your own eyes and really see how you had grown.

Now we are faced with the same problem again. You already know some of the ways in which having a license has changed your life. It will take a little time before you understand how being able to drive has changed you.

As the driver (and soon the owner) of a car, you are a different citizen than you were yesterday. You have a new status, a new meaning, and a new potential impact on the community in which you live. You are no more just a boy who drives than a husband is merely a bachelor with a wife.

Although this is the greatest single change that has taken place in your life to date, you can't look in a mirror and see it. It is a change in status, not physique, and you will have to feel it in your mind and heart. Until you do, we will probably have our troubles. Often, I suppose, I will be talking to the man, but you will hear me as the boy.

I think I have a good example of the problem we face.

A few months ago, when you were nearing sixteen, you and I and your friend Ralph were in our living room. We heard a siren and, looking out the window, we saw the police chasing a car along the highway. The three of us spoke at once. I said, "I hope they catch him." You and Ralph said, "I hope he gets away."

My immediate, instinctive reaction was on the side of the police, whom I regarded as the protectors of the community to which I belonged, as my protectors—and yours.

Your immediate, instinctive reaction was that of a boy to whom authority meant something that was imposed on one by adults, whether it be police, parents, or teachers. And, as a boy of almost sixteen, you were in the midst of your natural revolt against all these restrictive adult forces.

The two incidents I have mentioned are harmless enough, because they happened when you were a boy. But when you drive out as a man behind the wheel of your car, you cannot afford to carry as passengers your former childish attitudes of revolt, hostility, and aggression. As of today, as a driver, you have become a part of this adult society, and it is no longer something "up there" or "out there" that belongs to big, old strangers.

Now, to all boys under sixteen, you are one of us.

IV

You'll Have the Car Home by Ten

WELL,
here you are—a man when you are driving a car, and a boy when you get out. As your father, what am I going to do, if anything, about directing or controlling the "man" part of your life?

21

I imagine I will intrude less than I think I should, and more than you think I should.

Frankly, you and I are going to tangle many times about your behavior with and toward cars. And there are going to be times when, if I can't convince you I am right, I will pull my rank and insist you obey me, whether you agree or approve or not. I would rather have you boiling mad because I underestimated your maturity and good sense than in trouble or dead because I overestimated them.

One of the things I have tried to get across when we have argued about your conduct in the past is that I have two responsibilities in connection with you.

My first responsibility is to see that you are protected from any and every kind of harm from any and every source.

My second responsibility is to make sure the community is protected from you.

Now that you are a driver, my responsibilities become acute.

You may be impatient and irritated with my worries about your safety in a car, and grumble or snarl at me to leave you alone. I won't leave you alone, because that is only one side of it. I am equally concerned about the annoyances, damage, destruction and death you are capable of inflicting, with your car, upon the community and your fellow-citizens.

So, if the combination of youth and horse-power turns you into a squirrel, a show-off, a reckless or belligerent driver, careless of rights and lives, I will be less forgiving than God or the police courts often are.

As long as you live under my roof, I will not allow you to be a threat to your own or any other life with your car, any more than I would allow you to be such a threat with any other dangerous weapons. I will not be a "good guy" in order to help you commit suicide or murder. If you ever think it is "chicken" to drive carefully to protect lives, you had better be chicken to retain your right to drive.

Now don't get indignant. I am not denying you the right to have an accident, or even run afoul of the police. These are almost the normal hazards of driving, and can happen to anyone. I don't expect you to be perfect in any other aspect of your life. And even a perfect driver can be the victim of another's mistakes. Certainly, I must allow you to make some errors of inexperience or immaturity, even if they are serious ones.

When you drive, you are continually called upon to make sudden decisions that require judgment as well as skill, and you won't always judge correctly. No one does. And sometimes, a mistake can result in an accident or an arrest.

What I concede to you is the right to be wrong while trying to be right. What I cannot allow is for you to think you have the right to be wrong. There is a difference.

In the courts of this country, an accused man is presumed to be innocent until proven guilty. You deserve the same right as a driver. On the basis of present evidence, I consider you a good, trustworthy driver. If, through your actions, you prove me wrong, I will lower the boom.

Physical safety is only half the problem. The other half is the question of serenity. And I do not mean my own peace of mind.

I don't know why, but it is twice as much fun for a teen-ager to drive around town after midnight than before. But, after midnight, you and your car and your companions, cruising the town in a safe and sane manner, acquire the same nuisance value as somebody else's dog barking at that time of night.

This dog might be tied to a post, and harmless, but at two in the morning, to people trying to sleep, his bark is certainly worse than his bite. And I think you will agree that it is the decent duty of the owner to take his dog inside.

Now you know why, although I trust you, and there is nothing reckless about your driving, there is going to be a definite time when you and the car must be home. And I am sure there will be other times when, for my own fatherly reasons, and to your disgust, I blow the whistle on your use of a car.

I don't expect you to cheer when I clip your automotive wings for reasons that make no sense to you. But I intend to be the kind of young driver's father I think it my duty to be, whether you see my side of the argument or not. I will always try to explain my position, but I will not abandon it if I fail to win you over. There will be times when I am ruled by feelings, not mere facts; when the best "reason" I can give is, "Because I'm your father and I say so." And you will have to respect my wishes and obey.

V

Everybody Trusts
a Teen-Age Driver

Just before
you got your license, I asked you to define driving. You said it was the ability to control and
direct the movements of an automobile under
all possible driving conditions.

I agreed with you. But after thinking it

27

over, I think we were wrong. What we really had was a definition of operating an automobile, and driving is much more than that.

Driving is an act of faith.

Whenever you drive, you are demonstrating your faith and trust in untold hundreds or thousands of human beings you do not know, and they are demonstrating their faith in you.

Whenever you drive, you are betting your life that these untold and unknown masses of strangers can be trusted to drive on their own side of the road, stop for red lights, yield when you have the right of way, and obey all the other traffic rules. You are betting your life on the honesty and decency and courtesy of strangers.

If we couldn't trust our lives to 99 per cent of the people who drive, we would never get behind the wheel. The personal risk would be too great, and the insurance costs more than we could pay.

Most of the time, when there is an accident, there is also proof that someone broke faith and cheated. Improper passing, running red lights, turning without a signal, reckless driving—all these are examples of how people cheat and cause disaster.

But that is only the beginning. It may be that *every* accident is the result of someone cheating and breaking faith. This includes accidents that result from ignorance, lack of judgment, carelessness, inattention, or lack of common sense, what you might call passive, rather than active cheating.

Lets look at a very common type of accident that happens in many states. The road is straight and clear. The driver takes advantage of the straight, empty highway to open up, to "burn out the cobs." Traveling at high speed, the car suddenly runs off the straight road and the driver is killed or injured.

Later, investigation reveals that the accident happened because a tire blew, a part of the running gear broke, brakes seized, a bearing froze, or that the car "suddenly went out of control." Cause of the accident is listed as mechanical failure, and the driver inferentially cleared of blame.

But in ninety-nine out of a hundred accidents due to "mechanical failure," the driver *was* to blame.

The fact that a car can attain a speed of over a hundred miles an hour does not mean it can be *driven* at that speed. Our roads—even the straight ones—are not engineered to handle that speed. Our factory-produced cars, with few exceptions, are not designed or assembled in a manner to handle this speed. And few drivers, even with the best of roads and cars, are competent enough to drive at that speed.

When an ordinary driver, in a factory production car, drives one hundred miles an hour on a public highway, he is cheating. He may not be violating any traffic regulation, and he may be giving all his skill and attention to driving. Yet, he is cheating when he expects the road, the car, and himself to contain his speed. And if he loses control because of a flaw in the road, the car, or his skill, you can't blame mechanical failure or road conditions for his injury or death. It was a case of the driver cheating on the cold hard facts of driving life.

The act of faith you perform when you drive is more than obedience to traffic signs, and more than a trust in the people you meet.

It is also an act of faith in your own integrity, intelligence, and understanding of all the factors involved in good driving.

Just as you have to trust your life to the honesty, skill, and judgment of strangers, so must they, when they drive, put their lives in your hands on advance faith alone. Think of this when you drive. Each car you meet and safely pass represents one more human being who has staked his life on your respect for the law and on your skill and judgment.

Think about this when you are on the open road alone and are tempted to ask more of the road, the car, or of yourself, than one or more of you can honestly be asked to provide.

When you understand and respect the limitations of a situation that has no visible or legal limit, you can regard yourself as a good driver in every sense of the word. For then you will keep all the public and private faiths that are placed in you when you get behind the wheel.

Are you going to be the kind of driver who can and will keep these faiths of lawfulness, skill, and common sense? Time alone will tell.

Meanwhile, the human race is on your side. As of today, ten thousand people in this city, mostly unknown to you, are willing to bet their lives and the lives of their families that you can be trusted. What greater faith and trust could any boy ask from his fellow men?

VI

*Why Many Grandmothers
Are Better Drivers
than Their
Teen-Age Grandsons*

I HAVE
just finished telling you how much the world
and I trust you as a driver. If I meant what I
said, why do I keep on telling you how to
drive? Do I trust you or don't I? Besides, who
am I to tell you how to drive. We could prove

(on paper, at least) that you are the one who should be teaching me how to drive.

To begin with, you know a great deal more about cars than I do. For years you have read everything about cars and driving you could get your hands on. You know more about engine design, performance, modification and repair, more about suspension systems and problems, more about body construction and customizing.

Man to man, your vision is better than mine, your co-ordination smoother, your reflexes faster, your interest in driving greater, your I.Q. higher.

Finally, while I learned to drive catch-as-catch-can many years ago, you have been taught the driving art by a skilled instructor in a modern, high-powered car.

Yet, in every way, shape, and form, I am a better driver than you are, and I will be for some years to come. And for the same reasons, your mother who cares little about cars is a better driver than you are, and your grand-mother who cares nothing about them is a better driver than you are.

I am a better driver than you are because at the moment I communicate more fluently with the automobile than you do. After twenty-seven years and several hundred thousand miles of driving many kinds of cars under every driving situation, my experience makes me privy to driving confidences that are still denied you.

When I get into a car and drive it, the way it sounds, responds, and handles tells me more about the car than you are yet able to hear. The nature of the traffic I encounter divulges more secrets to me than to you. The personality, the pleasures, and the dangers of a strange road are often revealed to me the moment I look at its basic design, materials, quality of maintenance, and traffic stains or scars.

The best you can do at this time with any car is drive it the way you have learned to drive a car. I know better than you, at this time, through my hands and feet and the seat of my pants, how to amend my driving technique to suit the peculiarities of a particular car and according to the nature of the road or ground I am driving over.

For example, when I find myself on an asphalt road that was built during my childhood—and the design of a road reveals its age—I know I will find a road that is high in the center, with a rather steep slope to the edges, even in turns. On a left-hand turn, this means a road that is banked the wrong way, a turn that will do its best, should you hit it too hard, or at an awkward angle, or when it is slippery, to roll you into the nearest ditch, and which will resist your efforts to claw your way back.

Even now you can see and adjust to the obvious ways in which a bad road works against you instead of for you. But the obvious, individual hazards of an old road, like chuckholes, broken edges, and so on, are only part of the problem you face on it. The great danger to your safety is not the condition of the road, but its concept.

The new roads we build today are being designed for the future as well as the present. Most older roads were built to handle the traffic of their day. Much more important to you as a driver, they were designed around the cars of their day. For example, the grades on an undulating road were designed so that an oncoming car would be visible a certain safe number of feet away. But these grades were built for cars that were a foot or two higher than today's cars, and what was a safe design then is a dangerous one now.

When you take a car that is low, fast, with a long wheel base and slow steering, soft tires, and a cushiony suspension, and you drive on a road that was designed to carry cars that were high, slow, stiffly sprung, with hard, narrow tires, shorter wheel bases, quicker steering, your machine and this road are in constant conflict, waiting for an emergency situation to prove their unsuitability to each other. And until you have driven into and out of all kinds of driving problems on a road like this, and learned how you have to adapt standard corrective measures to the nature of the road, you will not be as good a driver on that road as those of us who have grown up with it.

These are some of the reasons why I am a better driver than you are. But the main reason I am better is that, while you have just learned to drive, I am still learning.

As you drive, I hope you will learn from your own experiences all that experience itself can teach. But the fact that we gain experience as we move through life doesn't mean we automatically learn anything from it.

I know of a boy who was driving his car at high speed one night with a girl as his passenger. They came over a little rise in the road and slammed into the back of a slow truck before he saw it. The girl was killed, the driver injured.

Several months later the same boy was on the same road at night, in a new car, and with another girl as his passenger. He decided to show the girl how the accident had happened, and took the same rise at the same high rate of speed. He hit another truck and killed the second girl. Again, he escaped with minor injuries.

There are drivers on the road who have somehow managed to live to a ripe old age despite their habit of depressing the clutch when they enter a turn and coasting around. And there are others who have driven for forty years without ever signaling a turn or paying attention to local stop signs. You and

I, driving out together, have often seen incompetent older drivers endangering the lives of everyone on the road. Experience, in their case, meant nothing more than many years of repeating their mistakes.

I think you will agree that what we learn from experience depends more on the nature of ourselves than on that of our experiences. And there is much in common between the young driver who can't be talked to because he has just learned all there is to know, and the old driver who can't be talked to because he has known it all, all his life.

You have had it dinned at you again and again that you must adopt a mature attitude toward driving. But what is a mature attitude?

In my opinion, it isn't merely a matter of obeying all the laws and driving carefully and thoughtfully. The mature attitude is nothing more than the willingness to continue learning. And, in driving, that means both the new things you can learn from new experiences, and the new things you can learn from the old, the familiar, and the known.

Above all, to become a good driver, you

must be a skeptic. You cannot drive by generalities. You must question everything, all the time, in the light of where you are, what you are doing, and with what car.

When you took the test for your license, you were asked how many feet it took for a car going 60 miles an hour to stop. The correct answer *on the test* was 171 feet.* That was fine for the test, but useless information on the road.

In how many feet can you stop a car going 60 miles an hour? Which car? With what kind of brakes? On what kind of surface? Going uphill, downhill, or on a level? Going an even 60, or in the act of accelerating or decelerating? And so on.

In how many feet can you stop a car traveling at 60 miles an hour? There is no answer to live by, to keep in your mind and drive by. The moment itself must tell you, based on car, road, and driving situation, how much distance you need. And as you drive and learn, experience will help provide the only answer that means anything to you—how much dis-

* Including reaction time.

tance you need, in your car, to stop *this* time.

Let's take another example of highway generality that must be viewed with skepticism, and that is the way many turns are posted with signs giving the "safe" speed. Safe for whom, in which car, under what conditions?

I have ridden with a racing driver who took me through a series of 45 mph turns at 95, without so much as making the car sway or lean. I have been with other drivers who couldn't take the same turns at 40 without using both sides of the road. These same turns, safe for the average driver in the average car on a dry road at 45, become entirely different problems when the road is wet or icy, the winds hard and erratic, of if the front end of the car you are driving happens to be badly out of alignment.

You learn to drive by questioning everything and applying every rule to yourself and your car and road conditions as you three are at that moment.

As you grow older, and as you drive more, will your car, will traffic, will the roads be able to tell you more than they can tell you now? Your ability to listen and learn from them—that is, from experience—may depend on your willingness and ability to listen to me now. Not because you are going to learn anything new about driving, but on the slim chance that you *might*.

VII
The Danger of Being a Careful Driver

Now let me tell you how you will probably get into trouble by being a careful, thoughtful, safe and sane driver.

You have assured me many times that you intend to be a careful driver, and I believe you.

I believe you will be as careful as you, *being you*, can be. The same way you are as neat, as thoughtful, as helpful and as courteous as you, being you at sixteen, can be.

The trouble will come from differences of opinion in defining the word "careful." What you think is careful, what I think is careful, and what the police think is careful, might be three different things. And in case of a tie, it is usually the policeman's definition that counts.

I have talked with some wild and erratic teen-age drivers, and each one of them thought he was, by his own standards, a careful, competent driver.

You have a friend who is now a civilized chauffeur, but who, just after he got his license, drove like a maniac. We live on a street that has many little children and no sidewalks, and this boy used to charge noisily down the street in his old car, skid around the corner and speed on, weaving from one side of the street to the other as he inexpertly fought the wheel.

At first the police and later his own maturity slowed him down. When he looks back at his recklessness, he is aghast. But at that time, he remembers, at sixteen, he considered himself a careful, superb driver. As he says, "I used to think people were looking at me and admiring my skill."

He threaded his wild way among the tots along the street, and thought the terrified parents not only approved, but admired him for it!

Is it possible for a reasonably normal, reasonably bright boy to delude himself to this extent? It is. . . . It is. . . .

Fifty times a day I see boys *and girls* disrupt and threaten the auto and pedestrian traffic in our town. They start up incautiously, race from corner to corner, weave in and out of traffic lanes, make fast, often illegal and uncontrolled turns, cruise slowly down the street side by side, talking and impeding traffic, bully other drivers, and ignore the rights of anyone else using the street.

Usually, when such young drivers are arrested, they seem surprised that their driving was considered reckless or careless. This is not an act; they *are* surprised. Most of them are convinced that however they drive, it is not, *when they do it,* careless, reckless, or incompetent.

I have heard you talk with friends, and I know you believe that getting your license and having a car are going to mean changes that they are not going to mean at all.

You believe that once you have a license and a car to drive, you will fly from the home cage on new wings of freedom, and you will have more control over your behavior and actions. You see in driving not only a freedom from my restraining hand and my authority, but freedom from restraint itself, and authority itself. You will find that the opposite is true. What you are in for is a life of greater control and more restrictions than you have heretofore known.

The fact is, you do not escape, you merely exchange. As you grow away from me and my control, you exchange one master for many, and you are very little your own boss. The father's "no" you shed at the home gate awaits you at every corner as the community "no." You will discover that while the freedom of being grown up means more freedom of movement, it also means less freedom of behavior than you knew as a child.

It may come as a shock for you to discover that you have punched your way out of a paper bag only to have punched your way into an iron box. You may resent finding so many new restrictions just as you seem to have outgrown the old. You may feel that obeying orders—even traffic orders—is a sign that you are still a child, that you have to show the world that you are big enough and man enough to make your own decisions and interpretations about the way you drive.

I have heard teen-age boys argue that, since they had better reflexes than older people, and were better drivers, they shouldn't have to observe the same traffic laws. That, for instance, a zone that is posted at 35 miles an hour for others, ought to allow a teen-age limit of 45 or 50, because boys could control their cars so much better. And that a boy driving at 50 could be driving more carefully than some older person at 35.

You haven't hit me with this argument yet, but I think you might be partial to it. That is why, although you have promised me that you will be a careful driver, the most I can expect is that you will be as careful as you, being yourself at sixteen, can be. And that is not enough to keep you out of trouble.

Your problem is not to be as careful as you now understand careful to be. It is to become, willingly and co-operatively, as careful as the community which gave you your license demands, whether you now agree with its rules, regulations, and conditions, or whether you don't. This was the promise you made when you accepted your license and the terms of keeping it.

This is nothing to fight against. To cling to your present level of understanding is to cling to yourself at the sixteen-year-old level, while every day brings you closer to seventeen. And what I call the community's definition of careful is nothing more than what your own definition of careful will be when you have grown all the way up.

That time will come more quickly than you

think. Already, I have heard you grumble that "something ought to be done to control those reckless fourteen- and fifteen-year-old kids on bicycles."

VIII
The Point of
No Return

TO PICK
up something I have said before, I think the
greatest danger that faces you as a driver is
that you, like so many others, believe good
driving depends on good vision and good reflexes; that since your reflexes are supposed to

be fastest in youth, you can safely drive in a more daring manner than older folks with slower reaction times.

This, to all practical purposes, is a myth.

The difference in reflexes between age and youth—if any—amounts to a matter of a split-second in any given individual. Not enough to make a difference in a critical situation.

There is an aviation term that every driver ought to know, and that is, the "point of no return." In flying, it is that point in a flight, just beyond the halfway mark, where if an emergency occurs it is a shorter distance to the airplane's destination than back to the home field.

In driving situations, too, there is a point of no return. It is the point where, no matter how skilled the driver, or how fast his reflexes, there is not time or space enough to avoid disaster.

If you were driving down the street at 25 miles an hour, and a child suddenly jumped in front of your car, the fastest reflexes in the world could not turn that car faster than that car, with its steering ratio, can be turned, nor could you stop that car in a shorter distance than that car, with its brakes, can be stopped at that speed.

If you should try to turn too fast on a glare of ice and begin to spin, there is no skill or reflex that can make up for the traction your tires need to bring your car under control.

Not only you. Not too long ago in England, the world's champion racing driver, twenty-nine-year-old Mike Hawthorne, went into a skid on a wet country road, crashed and died. Somehow, on an ordinary drive on an ordinary road, this most skilled driver, at the wheel of a sensitive sports car, passed the point of no return—and died.

The test of a good driver is not how he drives into—and possibly out of—dangerous situations. The test of a good driver is his ability to recognize the signs of road and traffic that indicate potentially dangerous situations, and to avoid blundering into trouble and past the point of no return.

I am worried about your safety in an automobile not because I doubt your skill or your reflexes, but because I think you do not possess enough of the "preventive reflex" that is essential to survival, nor appreciate its importance to you. This is not an individual flaw in you. You are weak where youth is weak, in that you are so aware of yourself, you tend to be blind to your surroundings. And you are weak where youth is weak in that you haven't spent enough hours in enough different kinds of traffic to recognize many gathering storm clouds of danger.

As you drive, you will learn to look for signs of possible trouble, and to be prepared for the unforeseen—and I *don't* mean the unexpected. There is a difference. You should always expect anything to happen, even those things which you cannot foresee.

To illustrate what I mean, let's take an ordinary drive across town, to see what has to be done to stay this side of the point of no return. Everything that is going to happen on this "drive" has happened to me at one time or another. There is no reason why they couldn't all happen on a single trip.

We walk out to the car as it stands in the driveway, then walk all around it. Just as I thought. The little neighbor boy has left his

wagon behind the right rear wheel of the car
—with his baby brother in it. We move the
baby to a safe place and cancel one ambulance
call we'd have made if we didn't remember
we have a lot of little neighbor children and
they have to be checked on before we back up.

We back safely into the street and start up.
Do you see what I see? Fifty yards ahead, a
mother is trying to catch a small running
child. They're on their own lawn now, but
where will he be when we get there? Just as I
thought. He's making a screaming dash for the
street, looking back over his shoulder. Don't
worry, madame, we've stopped and won't
start up again until you catch the little mons
. . . man.

Good thing we hand-signaled for a slowdown the moment we saw the child. That car
in back of us might have hit us if we had made
a panic stop without a chance to signal.

On again, and now what? We're overtaking
three boys on bikes, in Little League uniforms,
drinking Cokes out of bottles as they pedal
homeward down the middle of the street. If
we try to pass on either side without warning,

we might startle them into turning into us. Better give them a light touch of the horn, then wait to see which way they go to get out of the way. Just as I thought. One turned right, one turned left, and the third one hasn't decided yet. Good thing we didn't assume they'd all go left or right, and try to pass. The third one has moved over at last, and on we go.

Things look pretty clear now, but if you notice up ahead on the right side of the street, there's smoke coming from the tailpipe of the green sedan. That means the engine's running, and we'd better watch that car in case it pulls out in front of us without warning. Just like *that*. Never looked back to check before he pulled away from the curb. Good thing we were ready. Of course we had a warning. We were watching his left front tire. The moment he began to turn the wheel, we knew he was coming, even before he moved.

It's a good idea to watch those front wheels on oncoming traffic. The wheels always turn a fraction of a second before the car follows. Tips you off on sudden left turns, or helps you gauge how someone coming toward you around a turn is going to hold on his own side of the road.

Now we're in traffic, and watching out for the cars we ought to stay away from. The red one, making those erratic lane changes without a signal. Cutting in front of other cars with inches to spare. Watch out for him *and* the cars around him. If he piles them up, they're the cars we'll have to avoid.

Now what's this in front of us? Goes fast, then slow, then fast, then slow, weaves a little. . . . Young mother, it looks like, trying to drive with a young one loose in the front seat, a smaller one in one arm, a cigarette in her left hand. Looks like the bigger child is crying and trying to hit her. Maybe we'd better change streets before we do too. Can't count on her to drive with other traffic in mind. She doesn't know there are any other cars on the street. Don't depend on her for anything right.

Main Street. Traffic moving fast here. Watch out for that blue car. The baggage carrier is the first tip-off it could be a stranger. Out-of-state license proves it. Assume he doesn't know our street system and is just the one to make a sudden change of direction without warning. Why? He's on the left side of the street. The main highway turns right in two blocks. Sure it ought to be marked better, but it isn't. Meanwhile . . . there he goes! Aren't you glad we weren't trying to pass right about then? Good idea to give any car with an out-of-state license plenty of room. Figure the driver is both tired and lost, and apt to do anything.

Here's another one to watch out for. Car pulling a You-Rent-It trailer. Why? People who own and pull trailers are apt to know how to drive with a trailer. The guy who rents one for a trip may be pulling one for the first time in his life, and he might wrap it around your neck making it go left when he thinks he's making it go right.

Now what? We're moving in a steady stream of traffic, safely spaced. Somebody is impatient, and riding our tail. At this speed, he could never react and stop in time if we had to make a panic stop. No reason to let that threaten us, and only one thing to do . . . No, son, not try

to outrun him. Signal a slowdown. As we reduce speed, there's less chance of his over-
running his brakes. Good arm signal, and keep
it. There. We've opened up a space in front
of us, and here he goes around us to fill it
and ride somebody else's tail.

I'm not too happy about slowing down in
steady traffic and forcing traffic behind to slow
down, but it's the quickest way to remove the
threat of that rear-end smash. Why risk our
lives on *his* reflexes?

Now a series of downhill turns, double-lane
road. See that car in front of us? Little old
lady driver so short she has to look under the
rim of the steering wheel? Probably can't even
see the road. It would be legal to pass here, but
safe? See her swing into the left lane to turn?
If we were there, she'd be driving or knocking
us into the oncoming lane of traffic—or we'd
be scaring her into the ditch. I know, son.
. . . But she does have a license, and she is
driving, and it's not up to us to run her off
the road because she isn't a good driver.

Seen that car in the gas station driveway
yet? The convertible with the two boys. Five-

year-old car, but it gleams. What about it? He's getting ready to leave. Doesn't drive away from the pump, he guns away. So what? So he's just the guy to figure that if he doesn't stop for the highway the way he's supposed to, he can get on it before we get there—he thinks. And that's the way he played it. If we hadn't backed off a little, anticipating foolishness, we'd have hit. His car is in one piece now because we could tell he was stupid by the way he wore his hair. And I do believe he is muttering curses at us whenever he turns around.

Well, now he's found a brother. The tudor with the pipes, wheel covers off, and a crumpled fender. We can hear them both revving as they wait for the light to change. And away they go! Lucky for that late pedestrian he was between them when they took off. They're fighting it out neck and neck, but I do believe the race will be won by the black and white car with the red lights on top that just swung in behind them.

We're running along where the speed limit is 60, and the traffic is fairly heavy. Why am

I in the slow lane? Well, we're getting a light rain, the first in weeks, and there's a lot of oil mist on the road from thousands of exhaust pipes. And until there has been enough rain to wash the oil off the road, the mixture of oil and water will be as slick as grease. Some of those drivers sticking close together in the fast lane will find out what it's like if they have to stop in a hurry and expect their brakes to hold as if on dry pavement.

Another hazard when the road is like this, before people realize it's slippery: Watch those cars ahead when they start up at the green light, especially those making a right turn. Normal acceleration is too much for oil and water—look at them fishtail and skid. When it's like this, keep plenty of distance between yourself and other cars. Part of being a good driver is giving others a chance to make driving mistakes without mixing in.

Here we are on our way home. Our two right wheels just ran through a deep puddle. Expect the brakes to be wet and for the right side not to grab when the left side does. But don't wait for the time you have to brake.

We're alone on the road now. Put on a little light brake while you're giving the car the gas. Just enough to heat them up and dry them out. There . . . feel them taking hold evenly again? We're safe if we have to stop.

Back on our home street once more. See the two small children walking toward us on the sidewalk hand in hand? Mean anything to you? Well, when children walk holding hands, it's usually a sign they are going on a little walking trip, not just wandering and playing, maybe to that store across the street. Parents do tell kids to stay close and hold hands when going on an errand. Now they've stopped walking. Might mean they're going to change direction. That parked car has them hidden. Just in case, I'll signal that I'm slowing down and watch that parked car, and *here they come!* We really had to stand on the brakes for that one. Lucky we weren't going the legal limit, or we'd have hit them. Ran out right from behind that parked car, still holding hands, but not looking. Sure it was their fault for running out in the street, but **luckily it** was our "fault" they're still alive.

Well, here we are home again, after an un-eventful little ride across town. But there were a dozen times when we could have been closer to an accident than to safety—past the point of no return—if we hadn't acted to stay out of trouble rather than wait and react to it.

In a way what we just had was an example of defensive driving, and the technique cer-tainly seems simple enough. But I warn you now that no matter how much you want to drive defensively, it is going to be much harder for you than it looks.

Learning to read the signs of danger and trouble is only half the driving battle. It won't do you any good to recognize dangerous situ-ations if you are unwilling to avoid them. And it is here, I think, where most young drivers with fast reflexes have their accidents.

You are familiar with the physical law that a moving object tends to maintain its direction and to resist forces which attempt to change its course. Cornering with a car is a pretty good example of this law at work in your favorite sport. You can feel the weight of the car fight the change in direction.

The law seems to apply to the behavior of people as well as of things. We all have our dear habits, attitudes, prejudices, and ruts, and we usually tend to resist any attempt to make us change.

When we are in bed, we hate to get up. When we are up, we hate to go to bed. We resent having to quit some activity (like working on a car) in order to eat. Once at the table, committed to eating, we resent being called away before we are through. And so on.

As a driver, your danger isn't that you will fail to see possible hazards in your path, but that you will be reluctant to change your driving behavior to avoid them.

Somehow, in particular, it seems a great effort and imposition to take the foot off the accelerator and apply it to the brake. Once we are mentally committed to going in a certain direction at a certain speed, we resist and resent being forced to change our course and rate.

Somehow, in driving, it is easy to become so exclusively concerned with our own destination and desires that we are impatient with and annoyed by anything or anyone impeding our progress. It seems like a personal affront if we are stuck behind someone who is driving more slowly than we want to go, and as though our rights are being violated if we cannot pass the moment we want to.

In this, there is danger—danger of crowding too close to stop quickly, of making a sudden angry, reckless, "righteous" pass, of becoming so irritated at being thwarted that we lose both judgment and decency.

It is in this area that most young drivers make their most—and most fatal—mistakes. They are so jealous of their new "rights" as drivers, they are unable to change direction or behavior to be cautious and safe. Too rigidly, they commit themselves in advance to the way they want to drive and intend to drive, and fight any changes to the death.

Everything I have just said applies to adult as well as teen-age drivers. Yet, you cannot excuse foolish or reckless driving by claiming that "adults do it too." Not any more than the fact that some adults rob banks gives you some kind of legal excuse to do the same.

I want you to be an expert driver, but I am not very worried about your physical ability to drive a car or to make your way in all kinds of traffic. Let's face it—when you come right down to it, there is nothing very complicated or difficult about driving a car.

If the act of driving were a matter of high physical skill, we wouldn't have over eighty million drivers in this country. We'd have eight million, or eight thousand. At the moment you disagree with me, but that is because you have just learned to drive. As a new driver, you tend to exaggerate the skill needed to operate an automobile, because it is still a little strange and difficult for you. And, by exaggerating the difficulty, learning to drive becomes more of an accomplishment. But if your steering and reflexes and judgment are as good as those of the seventy-year-old ladies who drive thousands of miles a year without mishap, they will be good enough.

Your real test will come when the physical operation of the car is easy for you. Will you then be alert enough, and aware enough, to notice and read the danger signs of road and traffic? More important—will you be mature enough to act, so you will not be forced to react? Will you continue to be safe for others to meet on the road?

I am sure you think you possess the necessary qualities of good judgment, alertness, common sense and humaneness to be a good driver. Most drivers think they do; the worst drivers are positive of it.

Yet, even if you possess these good qualities and want to keep them, you are not out of danger. You have yet to learn what hidden emotions will be freed for the first time in your life when you become an automobile driver, that can sabotage the best of your conscious good intentions and carry you past your first—and possibly last—point of no return.

IX
Your Enemies Within

WHEN
I began talking to you about cars and driving a few years ago, I did my best to debunk the idea that cars or driving were exciting and glamorous. I tried to make you see the automobile as nothing more than a vehicle for

transportation.

I was wrong.

When you passed from being a boy on a bike to a young man in a car, you passed from a limited physical and emotional world into a world of thrills, excitement, glamor, freedom, and adventure, in which you have new definitions of time, distance, companionship, responsibility, and romance.

Along with the new freedoms and privileges and status of being a driver, come new emotional threats, which could not exist before you took over in the car. I want to talk a little about three major emotional traps that come with your driver's license, and how to avoid them.

You have been a boy for a long time, and like any boy, you are anxious to let the men know that you have come to join their ranks. And the most obvious way to do it seems to be with a car.

Once we get behind the wheel of our car, all distinctions of age or position between us and other human beings cease to exist. Climbing into a hot car is like buckling on a pistol. It is the great equalizer.

It would not be unusual if you felt you had to prove your new manhood with aggressive driving. It is only as a driver that you are allowed to compete with men as an equal, and it is only natural that your energies should go into proving yourself equal to any man. But to you, equal really means superior, and superior means driving better, and driving better means driving harder. And driving harder, when it is for this reason, means driving childishly.

Just as petty men have put to sea to glory in the absolute sovereignty of a small command, so petty men and defeated youths put out in cars to "prove," by recklessness and aggressive behavior, that they are to be reckoned with in this, if no other situation.

Is this what driving will bring out in you? Will the equality of the highway make you seek revenge against those you envy or feel socially or economically inferior to? Do you feel so personally without merit or worth that you need loud pipes and screeching tires to make the noise for you that cries, "I exist! I exist!" because you have no strong voice of your own? We will soon know.

I hope you don't fall for the notion that the road to maturity is the course for an Australian pursuit race, and that the only way you can become a man is by passing all the cars ahead of you. You can no more become a man by "outdriving" adults than I can become a boy again by beating teen-agers in a drag race.

The automobile is at once a source of joy and hazard because of its unique ability to match our moods and meet our emotional needs. When you are lonely, the car is a companion that can take you away from yourself to new sights and sounds. The purr of the engine, the responsiveness to your commands, the motion you desire, all provide a kind of mechanical companionship. When you are happy, the car is more than willing to sing along with you, to carry you lightly and happily to places and experiences that it helps make possible. And, when you are angry or hostile, the car will growl your threat as readily as it sang your song. It will, like a knight's

well-trained war horse, charge into any conflict or fray under your spur, and join you as
willingly in disaster as in triumph.

Once upon a time when you were little, you
reacted to disappointment and frustration by
throwing your toys on the floor or sulked with
a corner of your favorite blanket in your
mouth. Now you have a car to run to, and the
satisfactions of speed and noise and violence
that it affords.

And so, because the act of driving can so
perfectly mirror your feelings, you must watch
against "taking things out" with the car. You
translate your feelings into driving behavior so
subtly that your driving behavior can change
without your being aware of it.

If your girl turns you down for a date, you
are apt to express your resentment in the way
you drive. If your team loses a football game,
particularly away from home, you are apt to
"punish" that town by driving in a surly manner, ignoring the rights of others, and getting
some manner of revenge for the sports loss. If
you and I have had trouble, you are apt to

express your resentment against me by making life hard for all the adults you meet on the street.

Not only you. I know that when I have had a good day and drive home, I forgive the heavy traffic all its inconveniences. But when I have had a bad day, I resent every other car on the road and seem hemmed in by stupid drivers I can't forgive.

No matter how good a driver you want to be, you have to be aware of the way your mood will affect your approach to driving and the car, and not give in, not try to make the car an accessory to your hostile or unhappy feelings. It isn't easy, because when we are upset or angry, our ability to think and act is impaired, and our best judgment under stress is not very good. What you have to do is remember that emotional stress makes you a worse driver, and not to depend on yourself until you are calm.

Let's look at another threat to your welfare, no matter how prudent or sensible you plan to be.

There is always some oaf, thirsting for blood, ready to sneer "chicken" at a boy who drives carefully. Most of the time this is a boy with an established reputation for being a fool, anxious to prove that others are as stupid as he is. And he succeeds too often.

Again, it is the over-anxious desire to prove one's "manhood" that provides a willing victim. It is not easy to ignore a dare or a charge of being a coward, even from someone you dislike or despise. The natural desire to show up a challenger, to make a tormentor eat his words, easily leads you to become his prey, and perhaps sacrifice your life and the lives of others, trying to disprove a meaningless taunt from an ignorant source.

Partly this is true because we tend to develop strange loyalties toward our cars. We become so involved with the car that it seems a part of us. A disparaging remark about the car seems like a personal insult. We tend to identify ourselves so much with our cars that if some other car is faster, or corners better, or makes a louder noise, we feel that we have somehow been dishonored as individuals. I know it doesn't make sense, but that is the way it is. I know grown men who wouldn't make an issue of it if you insulted their wives, but who are ready to fight if you suggest they bought an inferior car.

And so, for personal and car-loyalty reasons, there will be times when you will be tempted to bet your life against a sneer, and it will take great moral strength to resist.

Now I want to talk about a third enemy to good driving within you.

What is coming up now is a rather strange little "facts-of-life" talk.

As you know, it is a common, not unusual thing for boys to postpone dating in favor of supporting a car. I have heard several of your friends tell you that since they couldn't afford both a car and a girl, they were giving up the girl.

There can be many reasons why a car is more important than a girl to a teen-age boy. The need for status, independence of movement, of feeling grown up, of being equal to other boys his age, are just a few of the more common needs satisfied by the car. But that is not all.

Many times I have heard many boys talk glowingly about the thrills of speed and the pleasures of hearing loud engines and exhaust pipes. These thrills and these pleasures seem obvious enough and innocent enough. But they can also be surface feelings that mask hidden, powerful, dangerous drives and forces within you.

I have read that teen-age boys taking psychological tests mentioned both speed and loud noises as being sexually stimulating to them. Here is the danger in your car. Not as a show-off sexual accessory, but as a sexual object. The danger that the car in loud, swift motion serves as a means of sexual stimulation —and, probably, a certain amount of gratification.

Is this why some boys can't slow down? Is this why they seem compelled to hurl their cars about recklessly, getting into accident after accident? Is this why they die at a hundred miles an hour, hurtling along in the grip of an impossible passion, seeking to force their cars to reach some impossible speed, in the tormented drive to reach, at some magic, ear-splitting rpm or mph, an impossible climax to an intolerable, perverted tension?

We warn boys and girls to be careful about kissing and love-making on dates, lest they arouse emotions they cannot control and "go too far."

I give you now a similar warning about your relationship with your car.

I don't know what emotional needs of yours this car will be called upon to satisfy. But whatever these satisfactions are, I warn you of the *emotional* point of no return. Search your soul to find out what driving and owning a car really mean to you. Be aware of the ways in which you can be lured through pride or passion into going too far and becoming the slave instead of the master of your machine.

I want to close this section with a few words that should help you handle your emotionally inspired driving problems.

Let me put it this way:

In our state it is legal for an adult to drink

alcoholic beverages, but it is against the law to expose others to one's driving when under their influence.

As a human being, you have the right to experience all the emotional drives, impulses, aggressions, desires, frustrations, and hostilities to which the human being is host. But you do not have the right to expose yourself or others to the threat of your driving while you are under the influence of negative, hostile, or immature emotions and attitudes.

It is just that simple to control yourself behind the wheel. When the day comes that you do it naturally, you will have proved, in a very quiet way, that you have at last become a man.

X
You and
Your Monster

As a seasoned veteran of movie and TV horror shows, you do not need my help in order to identify Dr. Frankenstein or his monster. You know them and their story well. But are you aware that you might be another Dr. Frankenstein?

Even now your monster—potentially much more terrible than his—sleeps in our garage, awaiting only a transmission, a clutch, a charged battery, and gasoline to bring it to life.

Soon, according to your plans, your monster will descend from its jack stands, sputter into life, and, with a roar, lurch from its cluttered lair to stalk among the local villagers.

Your monster has controls which you intend to operate. But the day your machine comes to life, will you control it or will it, as it already does in so many ways, control you? Who, I wonder, will enslave whom?

It is rather ironic that although the automobile is the greatest single threat to your physical survival, it is not physically that it is the greatest threat to your life. It is more dangerous to you morally, mentally, financially, and vocationally.

What is there about the *idea* of a car that not only appeals to boys, but charms them out of their senses? That blinds them to the true nature of themselves and the world as effectively as though their eyes had been poked out with hot irons?

It is something near, rather than something new.

Boys have always been the easy natural prey of daydreams, especially those that combine a life of adventure with all a fellow can eat. The vehicles of these daydreams change with the times, but the needs they satisfy remain the same.

Sixty years ago your grandfather left the farm to seek adventure and his fortune working on the railroad. Other boys of his time went to sea, or headed west to find excitement that paid wages, but willing to settle for work on the same terms.

When I was in high school, I reluctantly inhaled chalk dust and dreamed of an open biplane in which I, dressed in a long leather coat, breeches, boots, helmet and goggles, would barnstorm around the nation's pastures. I planned to attract crowds with spectacular stunt flying, then earn my fortune carrying the impressed country people aloft on short flights over their farms. What need for Latin or algebra in the life I planned, eh?

What I did about it was to run away from home and school with a knife in my boot and thirty-seven cents in my pocket. It was my plan, as soon as I became a barnstormer and had the necessary costume, to return and buzz the school building in my plane, discomfiting the teachers, astounding the other boys, and thrilling the girls with my feats of skill and daring.

For two weeks I hitchhiked, rode freight trains, slept in missions, and learned how long a teen-age boy could go without food and still live. Finally, not wanting to better my record in this area, I staggered into a police station and gave myself up for being a young fool.

You are the same kind of boy your grandfather was and that I was, but you don't have to run away to find your dream. The Aladdin's lamp that can make your dream come true is in our garage.

Without physically leaving home or school, it is possible for you, here and now, to board your sailing ship, ride your range, drive your train, or barnstorm in your old biplane. The automobile offers you, here and now, freedom, action, thrills, adventure, status, danger, and equality. With it, you can discomfit adults, astound other boys, and impress girls.

But that is not all.

The automobile also offers you an opportunity to earn your living in any one of a hundred ways. The automobile promises not only to be a romantic sweetheart, but a wife who can cook. What more could anyone ask? Why look further? Why waste time on the meaningless, non-automotive boredom of school-work? Why bother to investigate other careers?

You do attend classes, but the problems of working on your old car are much more important to you than the problems of your history or chemistry classes. Without leaving home or missing a day of school, you can run away from reality as definitely as I did when I stuck a knife in my boot and hopped a southbound freight.

I know you take a dim view of high school marriages. You think a boy is crazy to tie himself down for the rest of his life on the strength of an adolescent passion. Yet, you are willing to give up unlimited future vocational freedoms and opportunities because of an adolescent infatuation with the automobile. You are giving away the time, the opportunity, and the freedom to change your mind in the future.

What if, in a year or two, you change as you have so often changed in the past? What if you then cast off this spell, look at your coveralls and shrug, and are ready to give away your tools? What if, in a couple of years, you decide you have had enough of cars and want to go to college? What then?

What then, when you discover that the idea of the car has stolen not three weeks of your life, or three months, but enough of your youthful years and brains to keep you out of college and to force you back into coveralls, whether you like it or not. What then?

You assure me that you will always love, honor, and cherish automotive work, and I ask you this: Are you willing to bet your life on a teen-age crush?

You may not believe me after what I have just said, but I have nothing against the automobile as a hobby now or as a career later on. In fact, I think working on a car is one of the finest hobbies a boy can have at your age.

The hours you spend doing meaningful, constructive work on your car are hours that you are not wasting by standing around on street corners looking for something to do. Your car has given you an immediate, purposeful activity in life, a goal to work toward, and valuable experience in budgeting your time and your hard-earned money.

Work on your car has taught you more than a knowledge of mechanics and automobile construction. It has taught you patience, and has challenged your ingenuity and imagination. It has allowed you to dream creatively, then work to make that dream come true.

The time you spend under your car in our garage is good time. Knowing you are safe, happy, and constructive, I often bless the battered old car that "sits" for you so well.

I also think the work you do on your car will help make you a better driver. The more you understand your machine, the better you will be able to control it. The more of your sweat and effort that goes into building it up, the less likely you will be to abuse it, or break it down.

I suppose my argument hasn't been against the car itself, but against your going overboard about the idea of it. Because it really doesn't matter what sews your mind in a sack and dumps it in the corner. Whatever does, hurts you.

What I have said about the danger of an excessive interest in cars applies to any other interest that becomes an obsession and that tends to stunt your growth as a well-rounded human being. With others it could be girls, surfing, amateur radio, team sports, writing poetry, or even classroom work in school that engulfs too much of their young lives. With you, it happens to be cars. You are young and you are human, and what the car has done to others it can do to you. And this is what it has done and is doing to too many boys.

XI

Don't Drive Away from Your Generation

I WANT
to acquaint you with a sad pattern that is
common to every school in America. It is something that happens every day to too many boys
who become the physical and mental slaves of
their cars. It goes like this:

In order to satisfy his beloved car's demand for gas, oil, tires, rakish appearance, and hot performance, the boy who owns his own car looks for all the week-end and after-school work he can find. This doesn't seem like much time to spare. But, like the camel that begged to put just the tip of his cold nose in the Arab's tent, then pushed in and squeezed the Arab out, the automobile pleads for only a little of the boy's time and money then, inch by inch, usurps it all.

With his job and the work he does on his car, the boy has to give up athletics, school clubs and activities, and other less-important demands on his time.

Perhaps none of these school activities is important in itself, but something else is happening. By cutting himself away from extra-curricular activities, the boy cuts himself away from an important part of the purpose and meaning of school life.

School becomes a building to which he must report to attend classes. He becomes a stranger who sits in the classroom. The better hours and activities of being a schoolboy are stolen from him. Most deadly of all, he begins to lose touch with the normal life and progress of his generation.

Since the boy has divorced himself from the most interesting and pleasant parts of school life and associations, the limited, compulsory classroom side of school seems dull, meaningless, and foreign to his "real" life. The feeling of not belonging in school becomes stronger. His interest in his studies dwindles. He quits school in every way except that he attends.

No one likes to live on the fringes of society or to continue in a situation where one is a failure. There is little allure to remaining in school as one of the less successful students. A more pleasant picture is that of taking the step toward being a "real man"—to quit the classroom, to walk out on the grinds and squares and sissies, and to get a real man's job, and find a place in a man's world, and be able to drive a car that will make everybody in school turn green.

You have seen this happen in your school, and your school is one of many. Every day, all over the country, we lose a regiment of boys to the automobile in just this way. They may drop out passively, angrily, or with a happy shout of victory. But no matter how they have dropped out, willingly or by request, they have been defeated. They have failed to measure up to the standards of *their own* generation.

There is a cold, true fact to face. A boy does not belong in a man's world, doing a man's work. He belongs in a boy's world, doing a boy's work. That is his "real world." To continue in high school, and to take part in school activities, is the normal work of the normal child. To be thrown out, to drop out, to avoid participation (no matter how brave the excuse), is to fail and to fall behind your own generation. And if you cannot keep up with the march of your own generation now, your chances of catching up with it later are pretty slim.

If you let the car drive a wedge between you and your generation now, will you be any less a stranger to your people after ten years of exile? You have many roles to play in the future besides that of automobile driver. You will be worker, husband, father, and citizen. Each one demands a background of full participation and experience in all of life there is to be lived.

School (and I mean all phases of school life) is the engine that sets your generation into purposeful motion, that enables it to move in an orderly fashion toward the problems and the satisfactions of adult life. School is a window seat on this trip, reserved in your name. You can't afford to miss the ride or to make it boxed in a crate like a dog in a baggage car.

Where, what, and who will you be when your generation inherits the earth?

What precious years these are, and how precious few you have in which to prepare for manhood. Now is when you need all your senses about you, when you need clear eyes, an eager heart, and an open, curious mind. This is no time to let any interest, no matter how worthwhile, noble or exciting, shrink the size of your life and the variety of your needed experiences.

I imagine there is a terrible day that comes to all boys who, in particular, have let the automobile come between them and their youth, and between them and their future.

It is the day, I imagine, when the boy, grown older, looks around and sees what has always been here to see—that in this country almost everyone who wants a car has one. That old maids, and fat men, and housewives, and shoe clerks, and lawyers, and stenographers, and people with glasses, and people without hair, and people who never look under the hood, and people who just want to get from here to there, *all have cars!*

Look around you. Having a car is just about the most common ordinary thing there is about being an American. No one has to worry and dream and fret his youth away about *that*. As a matter of fact, it would be pretty hard to grow up and get a job and avoid owning a car. You can't turn around without someone trying to sell you a car—or, if you have one, a second car. All it takes to own a car, or play with a car, or fool with a car, or drive a car, or race a car, is the desire to do so, *and the money*.

You are going to be a boy for five more years. You will be an adult with a job and an income for forty or fifty years. What's your hurry?

That's not all. The worst is yet to come. I have seen it happen in our town.

The boy who quits school to support his car, or to get a better car *now*, soon discovers another painful truth. The boys who studied, who took part in school life, who went on to college, who put future first and transportation second, also have cars. And not only do they have cars, but their better jobs give them a better choice of cars!

It happens that way. In a few short years the boy who quit school to mortgage himself to this year's fanciest model car is still harnessed to a shabby, has-been automobile. The boy who could let cars wait until he became something himself is the one who can afford to compete on the drag strip, build up a better street machine, or take his choice of sports cars—all without sacrificing one minute of his own life.

One more thought on this subject: More than once you have accused me of being bound to the past. I warn you—don't bind yourself to your present self or to this present world.

You assure me you will always be interested in cars. Perhaps. But what if there aren't always cars to be interested in? I imagine there were boys who believed that fast horses and rakish buggies would never go out of style or be supplanted. And all the time Henry Ford and the others were working . . . working . . . working. . . .

This world of ours is moving ahead at breakneck speed, shedding old skins with every step. In a few years the automobile might be a relic of the past, replaced by some means of personal transportation as yet undreamed of. If you trade your life for a car now, where will you be then?

That is why I say to you: Like cars all you want to, enjoy them, work on them, fool with them, drive them for pleasure, and plan, if you wish, to drive them for profit. But leave yourself an "out," and don't get married to the car in high school.

I know what I have said sounds unsympathetic, and you feel I don't understand what it is like to be sixteen. There is a great deal I don't know about being sixteen that you know, but there is one thing I know that you don't. What I know about sixteen that you don't is what it is like to be seventeen.

XII
Living in a World You Made

DO YOU KNOW who is responsible for most of the bad teen-age drivers?

Good teen-age drivers.

Do you know who is creating tomorrow's bad adult drivers?

Today's good teen-age drivers.

Not long ago I played golf with three college boys who disclaimed any responsibility for the condition of the world today because it belonged to somebody else. "I was born," one boy said bitterly, "into a world I never made."

Whereupon the boy dropped an empty pop bottle on the fairway, thus making the world a worse place to play golf in for the people behind us.

No one ever was born into a world he had made beforehand, but each one of us helps make the world we are living in and will live in.

We do not live in the best of all possible worlds, but we do, in this country, live in the best of all available worlds. And, as a driver, you have a great deal to say about what kind of world is available to yourself and others.

What is the "world"? To the little children on our street, it is the street they live on. The way you drive back and forth along that street will do much to determine whether these little children live in a safe or in a dangerous world;

whether their parents live in a world free of, or filled with, fear.

The way you drive will determine, a hundred or a thousand times a day, what kind of world other drivers live in the moment they meet you. If you should destroy another driver, you not only change his *world*, you also change the kind of world his family lives in; you can alter the course of a dozen lives. You can make what had been a world of happiness into a world of despair.

I know you feel that, as a new driver, you enter a driving world that was made by people before you. But you and your generation are also and already responsible for making your world what it is.

For example, why do you think that the insurance you have to pay for your car is three times higher than the insurance rate I pay on mine? Why does this increased rate apply to teen-age boys, but *not* to teen-age girls?

This increased rate was not guessed at, set, or "made" by the insurance companies. It was made—and is still being made—by the way boys and young men drive today; by their accident rate; by the way they have chosen to make their world.

Teen-age drivers represent 3 per cent of the driving population, but they are responsible for 15 per cent of the accidents. This figure has held for years, and a company that insures a teen-age driver knows that he is about five times more likely to have an accident than are his parents. Since even a small accident can involve claims of several hundred or several thousand dollars, even the increased rate that teen-agers pay does not equal the amount of damages paid out in their behalf. Most insurance companies insure teen-agers more as a courtesy to their parents than as a matter of good business. To be good business, your rate would have to be many times higher than it is now.

But believe me—if, in a couple of years, the accident rate for teen-age boys dropped, so would their insurance premiums. I am not guessing. It has been proven that boys and girls who take driver training have fewer accidents than those who don't. As a result, many —perhaps most—insurance companies reduce their premiums for young drivers who have graduated from driver-training courses. And these people (you among them) have with training and care made this a less expensive world for themselves to live in.

Now to get back to my opening statements: It is not only the bad teen-age drivers who are responsible for their accidents and higher insurance rates. You and the other good teen-age drivers have to share the blame.

You have to share the blame because a feeling of "teen-ager loyalty" against the adult world prompts you to protect the bad teen-age drivers, to shield them from the police, to wink at and even admire their acts of bravado.

Because you are all teen-agers and imagine yourself in conflict with adult society, you admire the boys who outrun the police, who tear out clutches and transmissions in drag races, who have rolled cars or walked away from collisions. The good teen-agers all know what the bad ones do, where they do it, and when. But teen-ager loyalty seals all mouths.

You pay for it. You pay for it in being "picked on" by the police, and you pay for it in the form of high insurance premiums now. This is your reward for your loyalty.

This is only the beginning.

Not many years from now, you will discover that this loyalty to the irresponsible teen-age driver has created an adult problem. You are creating, for the time when you are an adult, a future army of adult careless, reckless, dangerous and drunken drivers.

I say you are creating them because you and your friends tolerate and even admire the reckless driving of fellow teen-agers. And if you give them the idea that their recklessness meets with the approval of their contemporaries *now*, they will grow up to be lawless thinking you will continue to admire them for it *then*.

This is the way you help make the world you live in today and will live in tomorrow. And right now, you are spending an extra hundred dollars a year to buy poor drivers the right to make this a worse world than it could be.

I suppose you wonder what I expect you to do about it. Do I want you to go around and "rat" on the bad teen-age drivers everytime they break a law? I don't know. Would you want me to keep silent if I saw a grown man commit a crime, on the grounds that we were fellow adults?

I think a better answer than turning careless drivers in, is turning them away. Most of them are driving recklessly because they want to impress their fellow teen-agers and have no real talents or accomplishments to win recognition. When their bad driving earns your contempt instead of your attention, their driving will get better. You, not they, must be the first to mature.

You must remember that all it takes to get a driver's license is the ability to pass a written test, a driving skills test, and a vision test. There is no test to determine the emotional ability of any person to handle a car. There should be, and I hope your generaton will provide it if mine doesn't.

That means that a number of reckless drivers aren't bad on purpose, but because they are not mentally or emotionally capable of accepting all the responsibilities of driving. When you who are normal protect, admire, and encourage these drivers in their recklessness, you

are more responsible than they for the accidents they have and the suicides or murders
they commit.

I say "you" are responsible. I should be more
fair. "We" are responsible. "I" am responsible.
You and your generation because you encourage bad drivers; I and my generation because
we tolerate them.

Despite the power we have to do so, only a
few areas in this country have acted to protect
the community from the incapable and the
incorrigible, and to protect the incapable and
incorrigible from themselves. Their lives, no
matter how foolishly they may want to live
them, are as precious as our own. It is our duty
to them as well as ourselves to deny them the
right to drive in order to protect their and our
right to live.

Whether you want to or not, like it or not,
admit it or not, you are, merely by being alive,
helping make your part of the world the kind
of place it is to live in. With regard to driving, how can you make it better?

You can begin by being the best possible
driver.

You can begin, as many boys interested in cars have already done, by joining with other boys in car clubs that have high standards for both cars and drivers.

You can begin by denying the bad, rebellious, immature or incompetent drivers your attention, admiration, protection or encouragement.

You can begin, even now, alone or with your friends, to petition the lawmakers to expand the testing of drivers, and to improve upon present laws and law enforcement.

If enough of "you" could do this and enough of "us" could do this, we might be surprised at how soon we'd find ourselves living in a better world that we made before we were born into it.

XIII

Be Commander-in-Chief of Your Car

SINCE MORE
Americans have been killed and wounded in
their cars than in all the wars this country has
ever fought, I think it would be helpful to
approach driving as though it were a military
problem, and to discuss it in terms of strategy

and tactics.

The dictionary defines *strategy* in part as, "the science and art of military command, exercised to meet the enemy in combat under advantageous conditions. . . ."

Tactics is defined in part as, "the science and art of disposing and maneuvering troops or ships in action or in the presence of the enemy."

In warfare, battles are fought with the tactics decided on by the strategists.

In driving, too, there is a similar separation between tactics and strategy. Tactics represents *how* you drive. Strategy (or lack of it) decides *why* you drive that way.

If your strategy—your understanding of the problems of driving—is poor, you will not be a good over-the-road (tactical) driver.

On the other hand, merely knowing what to do won't be enough if you haven't the skill or courage or equipment to put that knowledge into action.

There is no way I or anyone else can drive your car for you. Once you are behind the wheel and the car is in motion, you are in complete tactical command, and it is up to you, and you alone, to meet each driving problem or threat.

What I think I can do here, is help you develop a theory, a strategy of driving to help you "meet the enemy in combat under advantageous conditions." From then on, it is up to you.

1. *Always Look for Trouble in Your Car*

The best drivers I know are always looking for trouble. As they drive, they constantly and automatically try to anticipate every possible mishap or threat, and to have a plan of action in case the worst comes true. If a tire blows, if the steering suddenly fails, if that truck ignores the stop sign, if the oncoming car veers to the wrong side of the road, if the car in front goes out of control . . . All the time, these drivers try to be prepared for anything, and to have a way out figured before it happens. I will give you an example of this in action.

Some time ago a friend of mine, who is also a skilled pilot, was driving across the state in

a car of rather low power. He came up behind a truck and, seeing there was room to
pass, he pulled out and started by. The truck
increased its speed, and before he could pass,
he saw another car coming toward him.

Had he been driving a high-powered car, he
could have gotten around the truck with a
quick burst of speed. Knowing his car and
knowing he couldn't, he did the "right" thing.
He dropped back to pull in behind the truck.
Then he discovered that several cars following
him had tucked in tightly behind the truck,
and there was no place to go. So there he was,
stuck out on the wrong side of the road with
a car coming.

As a pilot who flies a small, single-engine
plane, he is in the habit of constantly watching the ground below for emergency landing
areas if his engine should fail. The habit came
to his rescue. He did the only safe thing that
could be done—and he had courage and skill
enough to do it safely. Instead of trying to
force his way back into the line of cars on
his right, he noticed that the ditch on the left-
hand side of the road was shallow, and he drove

across the road and into the ditch before the oncoming driver was close enough to get panicky. When the danger was over, he drove back on the road and continued on his way.

This habit of anticipating trouble, and of looking for the best way out should it happen, and wherever it happens, is the best over-the-road lifesaving technique I know. It is good strategy for survival, should you be skilled enough to employ the tactics it calls for.

2. *Never Make a Bet You Can't Afford to Lose*

You are waiting to cross a street or highway, and there are cars coming from the right and/or left. When is it safe to go?

In that situation I always ask myself one question. Instead of asking, "Can I make it?", I ask, "Can I afford *not* to make it?"

If my car—as cars sometimes do when put under sudden load—should hesitate, buck, or stall, would the drivers coming at me from either side have time to stop or turn aside before they hit me?

If I can afford to stall safely in the middle of the road, I go. Just how much margin I think I need depends on the road surface, the speed of the other cars, and the time I think it would take the other drivers to notice, then to react. And believe me, I am always generous with the amount of time I allow them.

This is also a pretty good rule of thumb to follow when you want to pull out to pass a car on the highway and other cars are coming toward you at a safe(?) distance. More than once, I have had a car that was cruising smoothly suddenly lose everything it had when I put my foot in it.

When in doubt, don't move out.

3. *Always Drive Your Own Car*

If you are traveling far enough behind the car ahead to stop when he stops, you can lull yourself into a sense of false security.

When you depend on his brake lights you are, in effect, letting the driver ahead drive your car, and you put yourself at the mercy of his reactions. For all you know, you are depending on the judgment of a fool, a drunk-ard or a daydreamer, who may lead you to disaster without ever touching his brake. This is one way you get chain reaction collisions.

I prefer, when possible, to take up a position that enables me to see something of the road ahead of the other car, so I can, if necessary, take a slowing or evasive action according to my own judgment and the nature of the road.

When I was much younger, I used to be-lieve the way to drive a strange road at night was to tuck in behind a local car and follow it. Again, this means letting a stranger drive your car and hitching your wagon to a star that might be destined to fall.

In a situation like this, a good driver can cause you as much grief as a poor one. I remem-ber a night when a racing driver took me through a series of tight turns at better than 90 to demonstrate some cornering techniques. A less-skilled stranger who might have tried to follow us on the theory it was safe to follow a local driver, would have been led to disaster.

This rule also applies to situations in which other drivers prod you with horn blasts, and you tend to act on their impatience. Ignore them and drive your car your own way. Don't be blasted, crowded, pushed, teased, or annoyed into driving your car the way some other driver wants you to. Besides being impatient, he could also be drunk, crazy, or just a plain fool.

At the same time, don't fret about the way other people are driving if their techniques differ from yours. Their reason for driving their way might be just as good as your reason for wanting to drive yours. One car is about all any one driver can handle at one time.

4. Know What Your Car Is Like Today

Cars, like people, have their "good" and "bad" days. A change in humidity, or atmospheric pressure, or wind strength and direction, or temperature, can all affect the behavior and handling of a car in a matter of hours. The state of the fuel, the kind of oil, the condition of your plugs or carb jets—all these are almost capriciously variable. And in addition to

the many known causes of varying performance and behavior, there are days when, for
no reason that anyone can discover, the car
runs twice as well—or half as good—as it ran
the day before.

I drive my car to the office every day, and
it never drives the same. Some days it leaps
forward with the slightest touch of the gas
pedal, winds easily, sings tightly, and handles
like a dream. On some of these same days, on
the trip home, it starts hard, runs rough, howls
and screams in the lower gears without seem-
ing to move at all, and has no power in high.
On these days I fight my way home in a
clumsy car that doesn't want to run, track
straight, or go through a turn without wallow-
ing all over the road. An hour later I may have
my "good" car back.

Each time you go out in your car, you should
be sensitive to its current state of behavior.
Depending on the way it ran "last time," and
putting too much faith in it to be like that
again, may lead to a pile-up.

I probably don't have to tell you this, but
it is something you do have to remind yourself

about to remember. The performance of your car and its handling can be greatly affected by the addition of a couple of passengers.

I think one reason a number of vacation accidents occur is that men become used to the feel and performance of a car that carries only a driver. They load up the car with family and baggage, and, because it is a "machine," they expect it to be just as lively, accelerate as fast, corner as well, and stop as quickly as it did with several hundred fewer pounds to carry. They try to drive a car that, to all intents and purposes, they left behind them. And they crack up.

Be sensitive to your car's behavior and limits each time you drive, and adjust your driving to fit its performance. You'll both live longer that way.

5. Learn the "Feel" of Control

Very often, when the newspapers report an accident, they state that the car "suddenly went out of control," or that the driver "lost control of his car" at such and such a place.

Very often, I think, the truth is that the driver never had the control to lose; that he was, unknown to himself, driving out of control, and all it took was an emergency situation or a bump or a turn to prove it.

Most experienced drivers know by feel and instinct when the car, and not the driver, is in control. Very few if any green drivers know it unless the car is *violently* out of control.

Keeping this to highway driving, there are certain speeds at which certain cars traveling on certain roads become, for all practical purposes, uncontrollable.

The fact that the driver is at the wheel, the car on the road, the radio playing and everybody is happy, does not detract from the fact that the car, not the driver, is "driving"; that the car has passed the point at which it can be guided with pinpoint accuracy, or stopped quickly without being "lost," or swerved sharply without somersaulting; that the car is in a state of what might be called harmonic distortion, its balance destroyed, and at the mercy of chance.

When a car is in this condition, it is possible

for it to be driven for a hundred miles without incident unless the moment arrives where control is essential. Then comes the newspaper story.

To me, one of the most dangerous maneuvers in driving is *de*celerating from high speed. It is not gaining or even maintaining speed that usually brings disaster, but the attempt to slow down. Deceleration is a nightmare in physics. It confounds, confuses, distorts, and reverses all the physical forces that have governed the car to that moment. It is possible, in some cars at some speeds, merely by taking your foot off the accelerator to make the car swap ends, or roll.

My worst moments in driving have come not when I was trying to go faster, or even when making a panic stop, but when I have been careless enough to let a car pass the control point, and I had to ease it back down, under power, to keep it on the road. And when all my instincts, I tell you, were to take my foot off the gas and reach for the brake.

Frankly, I don't know how to tell you how to recognize the point at which the car is no longer yours. All I can do is urge you to be alert, and sensitive, and know your car well. Knowing it intimately when under fine control, I think you will have the hands to sense when it is beginning to drive you.

6. *Never Run from the Police*

If you think the police are after you . . . stop!

If you know you are guilty of a violation . . . admit it.

If you run into another car or object or human being, and there are no witnesses to the accident, it doesn't matter whether you dented a fender or killed a man—turn yourself in.

There are a number of reasons why you should never run from the police and why you should, if necessary, do the other things I advise.

First of all, whatever you are guilty of when the police come after you, you are really in trouble the minute you start to run.

At no other time are you more likely to have an accident or kill yourself and perhaps others. When you run you are frightened, and when you are frightened your senses are blunted. You cannot see as well, think as well, or control your actions as well.

We have had several local cases in which boys and young men, fleeing the police to escape a traffic charge, turned off their lights and sped through the city blacked-out at 90 miles an hour. One I remember was wrecked, and another shot.

The next time you are driving through town at night, safe and secure as you cross an intersection with the green light, imagine your position if one of those drivers was approaching the intersection with his lights out wildly running the red light at 90. Need I say more?

7. *Protect Your Reputation!*

There is another reason why you should never try to outrun the police, even more important than the reasons I have just given.

The boy hasn't been born who can outrun the police and keep quiet about it, and news like that gets *all around* the community in a very short time. Even if the police cannot act on this particular instance, they know who you are. More important, they know *what* you are. Even the friends who seem to laugh with you over your escapades know what you are: a coward and a sneak. They will laugh with you when you escape, but they will laugh at you when you are caught. And they will never, believe me, trust you.

I tell you to stop, to admit when you are in the wrong, to obey the law when no one seems to be looking, because someday your freedom might depend on your word—on your reputation.

Driving being what it is, there are going to be mishaps and accidents. Most of the time, each driver will claim the other at fault, and there isn't always material evidence to prove which one is right. Often, both parties honestly believe they were in the right.

If you should become involved in an accident, and your liability and even freedom depended on your word, that would be the moment when your chickens came home to roost.

If you have built up the reputation of a

driver who cheats, sneaks, evades, tries to lie his way out of trouble, and is contemptuous of authority and the idea of personal responsibility, you are lost.

If, on the other hand, you have built up a reputation for truthfulness, for preferring to be honest and punished rather than escape penalty by lies, your word, based on your reputation, will be your most precious asset.

Yet, how many, many boys will carelessly throw away a priceless reputation for honesty in the attempt to escape a small fine or reprimand?

A good or bad reputation is not something one "gets," but is something one makes. Your reputation represents you as you are willing to let others see you.

If you try to lie your way out of a jam, you announce your willingness to be known as a liar.

If you try to run from trouble, you announce your willingness to be known as a coward.

If you fail to report an accident because there were no witnesses, and later you are caught, you announce your willingness to be known publicly as a sneak.

The kind of reputation you make for yourself now, by your attitude toward the personal responsibilities of driving, is a kind of public preview of how you will probably face other coming individual adult responsibilities.

For your sake now, and in the future, I hope you never risk getting the reputation of a person who would lose all of his soul in the attempt to save a piece of his skin.

8. *When You Get Good . . . Watch Out!*

Although you have earned your license, you are still an awkward driver and unsure of yourself behind the wheel. Even so, I trust you more as a driver now than I will six months or a year from now.

As long as driving is new and difficult, you will work hard to drive right. When it gets easy, the way you drive will be "right."

Several months from now you will have it "made." You will drive relaxed and confident, often with one hand. You will handle your car deftly and certainly in every kind of traffic situation, all without stress or strain. You will corner expertly, shift smoothly and swiftly, and make all decisions instantly.

Watch out!

When I was your age, I worked at an airfield during the summer, and I learned something about airplane accidents that applies to driving. We had very few accidents among the older pilots, and very few among the student pilots. The critical period came several months after a pilot had soloed, and flying became "natural" to him, and he was able (he thought) to relax—when, I suppose, he felt like a better pilot than he was because caution itself had not become a natural flying habit.

This happens in driving too. After the tension of learning, the period of easy confidence sets in, when one feels like a better driver than he is; when the warnings and the dangers seem to have been overemphasized; when driving *seems* like . . . nothing at all.

It seems to me, as I read the vital statistics column in the paper, that more seventeen-year-old drivers are arrested for violations or involved in accidents than drivers of any other "teen" year. Perhaps this happens because seventeen is halfway between the learning period of sixteen and the mature caution that becomes normal at eighteen.

Whatever the reason, don't relax yourself into trouble. The minute you feel you have become a good driver—watch out.

A Final Word

As your father, your friend—and as a more experienced driver—it is hard for me to quit giving you information and advice about the strategies, tactics, and ethics of driving.

But if there is no limit to the amount of advice one wants to give, there is a limit to the amount of advice another one wants to—or is able to—get.

I think we have reached that limit. You may think we passed it long ago.

I have tried to help you be a good driver. You have been taught to drive by a competent professional teacher, and together we have discussed many of the problems that confront every driver, and especially young ones.

Now I can only hope that respect for the laws of men, courtesy, and physics will not desert you when you are on your own.

Unless you are alert and courteous and wise along the trails of your century; unless you survive the ambushes at the intersections and the inescapable skirmishes of the open road, life is in truth an empty dream and the grave in truth its goal.

The rusted iron in the ditch was once a car as sporty as the one you dream of; the boy they drag out somewhere every hour to cover and bury, was as fine and smart and loved as you.

Be gentle with your horses, boy, and get your wagon through.